Ian Applecat
Christmas in Sanoyea

**Written by
Ophelia S. Lewis**

**Illustrated by
Shabamukama Osbert**

VILLAGE TALES PUBLISHING

A Sapo Children's Book
Published by Village Tales Publishing
Text Copyright ©2019 by Ophelia S. Lewis
Illustrations copyright ©2019 Village Tales Publishing

A catalog record for this book is available from the Library of Congress:
LCCN: 2019909912
ISBN: 9781945408496

Cover Design By OASS

www.villagetalespublishing.com
www.oass.villagetalespublishing.com
www.childrens.villagetalespublishing.com

Dedicated to

My beloved mother, Jeanette B. Lewis,
my Awesome-Grandsome squad;
Elijah, Logan, London, Lydia, Ian and Liyah,
and all the children in Liberia.

Chapter One:
To the Farm

The children were looking forward to a fun Christmas, even though on Grandpa's farm in Sanoyea there would be no TV. Ian was happy to spend the holiday with his sister Lydia, his friend Little Bea, his dog Applecat, and his twin cousins, Nostelor and Nostelda.

The twins had come to Liberia from America for their first Christmas. Nostelda did big boys things even though he was only six years old. He also got into trouble a lot.

Nostelor was much less naughty.

Mama, Papa, Aunty Leemu, Uncle Flomo, and the children boarded the big bus to Sanoyea, Bong County. The children played guessing

games as they drove through towns and villages from Monrovia to Grandpa's farm. Sometimes the grownups joined them.

Grandpa and Grandma could hardly wait to hear their grandchildren laughing. They were happy to see the family arrive.

The farm was every child's dream. It had a big safe yard to play in and explore. The house was cozy and the kitchen smelled like warm rice bread. Grandma loved to bake rice bread. Besides

the space and food, the best thing on the farm were the animals.

Nostelda had never seen a live chicken. He wanted to see how fast they could run or fly. Luckily for him, there were some chickens feeding in the yard nearby.

"Watch this," Nostelda said.

He rushed toward the chickens. The chickens squawked, clucked, and flapped their wings. Some even pooped. A rooster said, "Coko-lee-oko!" The children laughed. Applecat barked and wagged his tail. Then a huge bird walked by with its large fan-shaped tail feathers.

"What is that?" Little Bea asked.

"That's a turkey," Lydia said.

The turkey's head was the ugliest thing they had

ever seen, with a fleshy red snood under its beak.

"I bet that turkey can fly," Nostelda said. He shooed it away, but the turkey did not run.

"Farm turkeys don't fly," Lydia said. "They are too heavy. Only wild turkeys fly!"

Nostelda ran toward the turkey and it took off.

He chased the turkey all over the yard. Grandpa heard the noise.

"Don't chase the chickens," he yelled. "Come here children, I want you to meet someone."

"This is Lono Kollie," Grandpa said. "He will be watching y'all."

Chapter Two:
When Pigs Lay Eggs

Sixteen year old Lono Kollie helped around the farm on the weekends and Grandpa paid his school fees. Lono Kollie brought a few hand-built toys to show the children. He had a ganga ball made from dried up rubber tree latex, a truck made from bamboo, and a slingshot made from wood. The strap on it looked like a fat rubber band.

"How come there are no dolls," Lydia asked.

"I'm sorry," Lono Kollie said, "I did not know there would be girls. I will make doll babies for

you later," he promised.

Suddenly small raindrops started to fall from the sky.

"Follow me," Lono Kollie instructed.

The children followed him to a big palava hut in the yard. Applecat picked up a stick in his mouth and marched along.

Under the mango tree next to the palava hut, Lono Kollie taught them about recycling to save the earth. All the materials used to build his toys were from something that had been either thrown away or came from a tree. He told them the slingshot was used to drive birds away from the rice farm, or sometimes to hunt small animals for food.

The children loved Lono Kollie. After the rain

stopped, Grandpa joined the group under the palava hut.

"Grandpa, do pigs lay eggs?" Ian asked. "They must be very big. Bigger than chicken eggs, I bet."

Grandpa laughed. "No, Ian, pigs don't lay eggs," he said. "Why would you think they lay eggs?"

"Nostelda said they're so big, I couldn't eat a whole one."

"Pigs do not lay eggs," Grandpa said. "They have baby piglets."

Nostelda promised to show Ian a pig's egg anyway. The others wanted to see it too, they all went to the pigpen. There were no eggs there, so the children decided to explore behind it.

Behind the pigpen was nothing but puddles and sloppy mud. The girls stayed back as far away as possible. Nostelda and Ian walked around the muddy puddles, trying not to touch it. Applecat ran pass Ian and walked right into the puddle, making paw prints in the mud.

"No, Applecat, come back," Ian yelled.
Applecat came running, wagging his tail. He

jumped to give Ian a hug and left muddy paw prints all over Ian's shirt.

"Applecat, stay with them while I go and ask Mama to clean my shirt," Ian said.

Chapter Three:
The Turkey and The Firecracker

Later, the children went to the house to get their treat bags filled with cookies, candy, popcorn, juice boxes, and peanut butter crackers. As they left the house, no one noticed the turkey. It targeted Nostelda and chased him as soon as he walked out. Nostelda ran back inside. Each time he tried to join the others, the turkey would run behind him and Nostelda would run into the house.

"I won't be able to come out to play," Nostelda pouted.

"I have an idea," Ian said. "If you wear Nostelor's dress, the turkey won't know it is you."

Nostelda loved the idea.

"What a clever idea," Lydia said, and hugged her little brother.

Everybody followed Nostelda to the bedroom. Nostelor gave him one of her dresses, and it fitted.

"Now, you can go outside," Ian said. "You look like Nostelor without cornrows. The turkey won't know it's you."

Everybody laughed. Applecat barked and wagged his tail.

To be careful, the children used the back door and Nostelda walked in the middle of the group. They took two steps outside, and the turkey ran towards Nostelda.

Nostelda ran away, but the turkey kept close. It was hard to get away from the fast bird.

Then, Nostelda's feet slipped. He was about to fall when Lono Kollie showed up.

In one strong leap, Lono Kollie grabbed the

turkey with both hands. Dust swirled in the air. The children cheered and Applecat barked. Lono Kollie put the turkey under his arm and took it away.

"What a clever turkey," Little Bea said, laughing.

"He is clever," Ian said, "but Applecat can do more tricks."

Everything had been amazing until the turkey chase. Lono Kollie met the children at the palava hut to do more fun things. He put his biscuit tin down and told them he would be right back.

As soon as Lono Kollie walked away, Nostelda took the biscuit tin and told the others to follow him. Everyone gathered around him when they

reached behind the chicken coop.

He opened the biscuit tin and pulled a box of matches from his pocket.

"Firecrackers," he said. "I know how they work."

"That's for Lono Kollie," Ian warned. "We are not supposed to play with it."

"I only want to show you what I saw on TV," Nostelda said. "Stand way back, everybody."

Everybody moved back.

Nostelda lit three matches, but the breeze blew each one out before he could set it to the firecrackers.

"Something's wrong with the matches," Nostelda said.

Lono Kollie returned to the palava hut, but did not find the children there. He did not know where they had gone. He ran to the pigpen, but they were not there either. On his way back to the palava hut, he followed the smell of burnt matches behind the chicken coop.

"What are you all doing here?"

"Nostelda was going to show us how firecrackers work," Ian said.

"You are not supposed to play with matches," Lono Kollie said to Nostelda. He sounded upset.

"I thought you wouldn't mind," Nostelda said.

"I do mind," Lono Kollie said. "Children are not supposed to play with matches."

"I'm sorry, Lono Kollie," Nostelda said. "I didn't mean to make you mad." He handed over the box of matches. "Please don't be angry."

"I'm not vexed," Lono Kollie said. "If you

promise never to play with matches again, I will light some firecrackers for you to see."

"Yeah!" Everybody yelled. Applecat barked. The firecracker's fiery sparks were beautiful and exciting.

Chapter Four:
That's Not Santa

In the distance an interesting sound interrupted the popping firecrackers. A dancer wearing a red and white straw skirt had arrived to Grandpa's farm with his troupe rattling bottles, beating drums, hitting empty tin cans, and playing a saw. The group was not the only one. Other cultural artists, like the tall and short dancing devils, also came to perform.

"That's not Santa Claus," Nostelda said, pouting.

"That's our Liberian Santa," Lydia said. "We

call him, Sanny Klos. Mama said they are cultural artists. They go from neighborhood to neighborhood singing and dancing."

"But, where are the gifts?" Nostelda asked.

"They don't bring gifts," Lydia answered. "People give them money when they dance."

"What? Give them money? I don't like the Liberian Santa," Nostelda said. "Santa is supposed to bring gifts. I like our Santa in America."

"It's not good manners to pout, Nostelda," Lydia said. "In America, does Santa dance?"

"No."

"Watch Sanny Klos dance."

The music started, and Sanny Klos began dancing. He moved like a ribbon in the breeze. Sanny Klos tumbled, and tumbled, and tumbled some more. He even spun around while on his back. Then Sanny Klos trembled and did a few back-flips. He rolled to and fro.

A little boy about Nostelda's age jumped high in the air and somehow landed on a man's shoulders. The little boy danced while standing there. He did all the dance moves the big boys did.

"Wow," Nostelda shouted, "Look at that. That little boy is cool. I like him. I really like him!"

"He's a tactic pekin," Lydia told him.

Nostelda ran to his mother.

"Mama, can I get my allowance now? I want to give it to Sanny Klos."

"I thought you did not like Sanny Klos," Aunty Leemu said.

"I like Sanny Klos, Mama. I want to be a tactic

pekin. I want to dance like that little boy."

The celebration continued all day long. Everybody ate a lot of jollof rice, potato salad, fried chicken, fufu and pepper soup, and other Liberian foods.

At the end of the day, Lono Kollie presented the girls with three stick-dolls. Then when night came, he lit the skies with more firecrackers. Christmas in Sanoyea was the best Christmas ever.

Ophelia S. Lewis (Author)

A mission to transform the limited books available with African characters in children's books today, drawing from her own childhood for inspiration, Lewis creates cultural-genre books with African characters all children can relate to. Of her work, Lewis says, "The best way of getting people familiar with the importance of identity and own surroundings is through the eyes of childhood. Start at the earliest stage of life." Learn more about her work at www.ophelialewis.com

Books by Ophelia S. Lewis
A is for Africa * I'm About To * Toby Pannoh's Good Manners for Boys and Girls * GMA (how to be a super polite kid) * Where in the World is Liberia * Aventures at Camp Pootie-Cho Game & Puzzle Activity Book * Keeping Secrets Adventures at Camp Pootie-Cho Good Manners ABCs

Shabamukama Osbert (Illustrator)

Since joining Village Tales Publishing in 2016, Osbert has done illustrations for several books by different authors; BALLAH MAKES SHAPES (Augustus Y. Voahn), TOBY PANNOH'S GOOD MANNERS FOR BOYS AND GIRLS (Ophelia S. Lewis), LITTLE BRAVE LYDIA and DRAMA ON PIPELINE ROAD (Nemen M. Kpahn), BETTER TOGETHER (L.M. Logan), and KEEPING SERCRETS (Ophelia S. Lewis).

Village Tales Publishing is bringing another first to its Children's literature division—Sapo Children's Books. We are excited to be launching two new children's series starting 2018 summer; ADVENTURES AT CAMP POOTIE-CHO and IAN & APPLECAT. As part of our Reading-Our-World campaign, these books are for age groups three-to-five years and six-to-twelve years.

Keeping Secrets (Ian & Applecat series - book 101)
It's fun having a dog, but there's nothing funny about keeping the dog out of trouble. Applecat has chewed Lydia's favorite book to shreds and could be sent away. Ian has to decide if he should Tell or Not. He loves his dog, but it's hard keeping Applecat's secret.

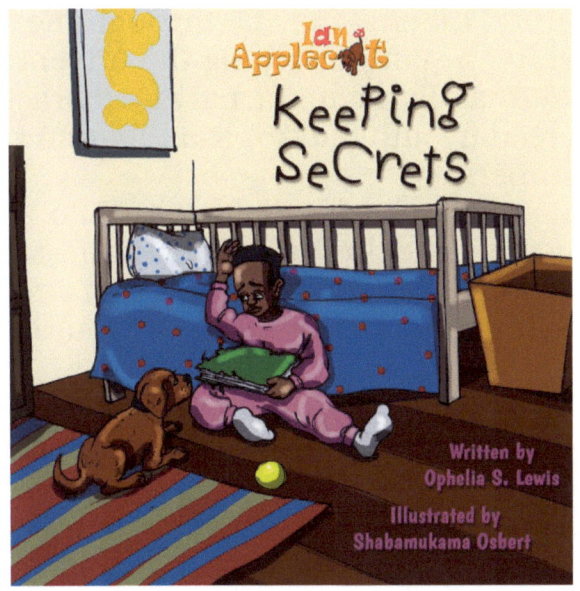

Series: Ian and Applecat (Book 101)
Paperback: 44 pages
Publisher: Village Tales Publishing (September 30, 2018)
ISBN-10: 1945408340
ISBN-13: 978-1945408342
Dimensions: 8.5 x 0.1 x 8.5 inches

Sapo National Park & Adventures at Camp Pootie-Cho

Since its establishment in 1976, the World Wildlife Fund, and World Conservation Union, among other international organizations, have kept up the efforts to maintain Sapo National Park, Liberia's prominent national park. Sapo National Park plays an important part of Liberia's survivability, along with its people; making it vital that we prepare future generations to lead Liberia with eco-conscious capabilities. One way of getting people familiar with the importance of Sapo National Park in Sinoe County, Liberia, may be through the eyes of children. In 2018, Village Tales Publishing began publishing the Adventures at Camp Pootie-Cho series using native animals living in the park as characters. "Adventures at Camp Pootie-Cho" takes readers into the tropical Liberian rainforest to learn from its special animal campers.

Our first book, **Better Together:** in this adventure, it's Field Day. Solo Dawg and Zaq Lyons become team captains. As they race through different obstacles, the campers must choose to move quickly or stick together. See which animals make it and which ones don't, in this fun story about teamwork. On your mark. Get set. Go!

Join us on our adventures at Camp Pootie-Cho! www.camppootiecho.com

www.ingramcontent.com/pod-product-compliance
Lightning Source LLC
Chambersburg PA
CBHW041001170626
46815CB00002B/101

9 7 8 1 9 4 5 4 0 8 4 9 6